CHRISTMAS MEDLEYS

CONTENTS

— PIANO LEVEL —
LATE INTERMEDIATE/EARLY ADVANCED

ISBN-13: 978-1-4234-2673-8

HAL•LEONARD®
CORPORATION
7777 W. BLUEMOUND RD. P.O. BOX 13819 MILWAUKEE, WI 53213

Visit Hal Leonard Online at
www.halleonard.com
Visit Phillip at
www.phillipkeveren.com

PREFACE

I arrange numerous books for piano each year—pop songs, hymns, movie songs, classical themes. I enjoy them all. But there is something special about Christmas music, and when it's time to arrange holiday folios I am eager to the task. The funny thing is, however, that Christmas project deadlines tend to be in May or June. My family has laughed for years at the incongruity of Christmas tunes singing from my piano studio as the temperature soars into the 90s outside. It is a bit strange, indeed.

I tried something different this year. Just after Thanksgiving I began working on *Christmas Medleys*, just a measure or two as the Christmas spirit began to build. As the tree went up in our home, this collection of arrangements began to take shape. The writing of this book was part of the tapestry of Christmas 2006 in the Keveren family.

It was a very special Christmas. Our daughter, Lindsay, was home from her first semester away at college, which made it particularly sweet. "Christmas Reminiscence" was written as homage to the many holiday memories we share as a family.

May this music make your Christmas a little brighter!

Sincerely,
Phillip Keveren

p.s. Many of these arrangements are adaptations of settings I originally created for a recording, *Symphony of Carols*, featuring piano and symphonic orchestra (Discovery House Music).

BIOGRAPHY

Phillip Keveren, a multi-talented keyboard artist and composer, has composed original works in a variety of genres from piano solo to symphonic orchestra. Mr. Keveren gives frequent concerts and workshops for teachers and their students in the United States, Canada, Europe, and Asia. Mr. Keveren holds a B.M. in composition from California State University Northridge and a M.M. in composition from the University of Southern California.

AWAY IN A MANGER

Arranged by Phillip Keveren

"Away in a Manger" (James R. Murray)

Gently flowing (♩ = 88)

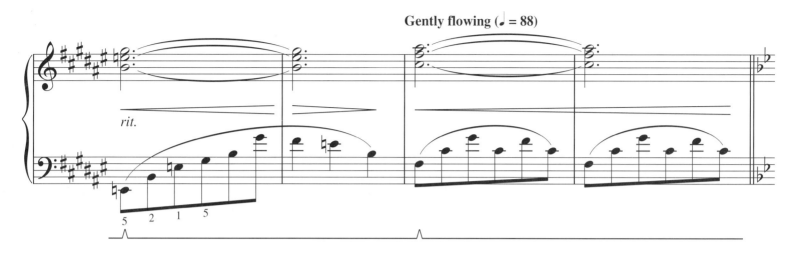

"Away in a Manger" (William J. Kirkpatrick)

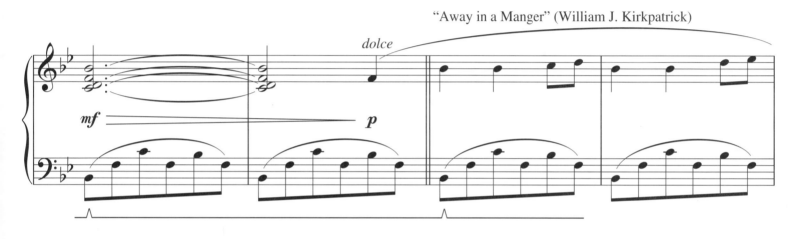

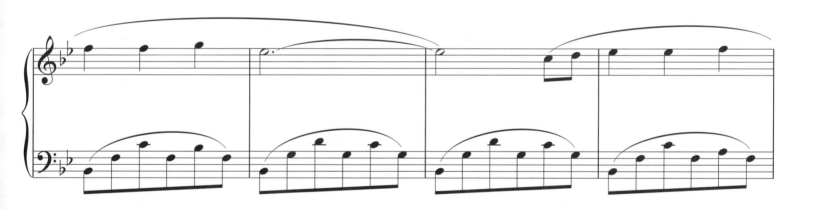

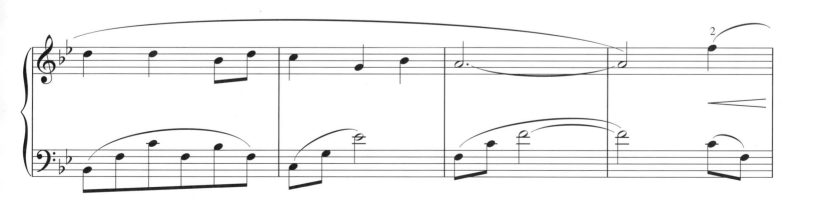

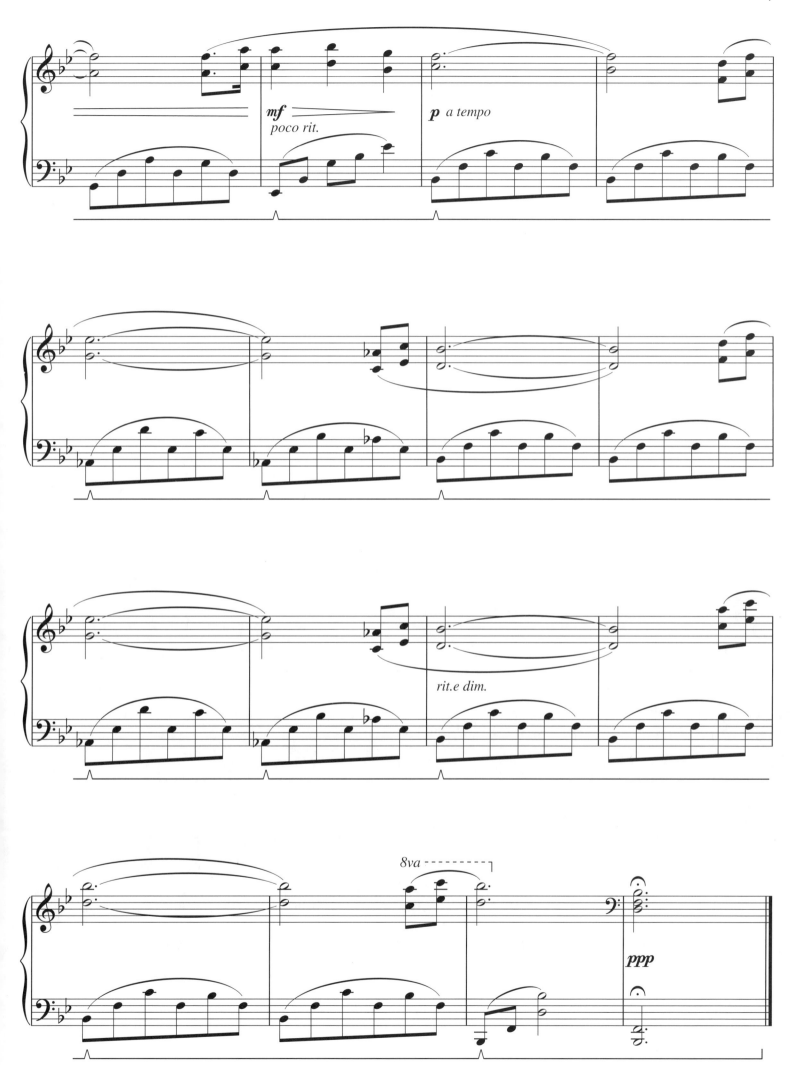

ANGEL SUITE

Arranged by Phillip Keveren

Flowing (♩ = 138)

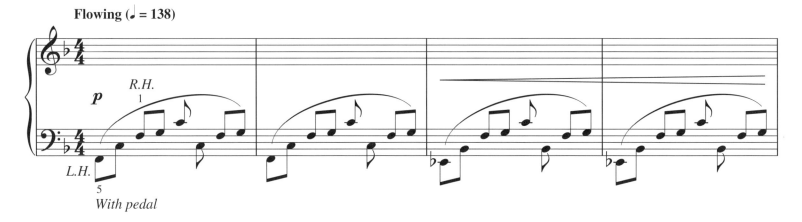

With pedal

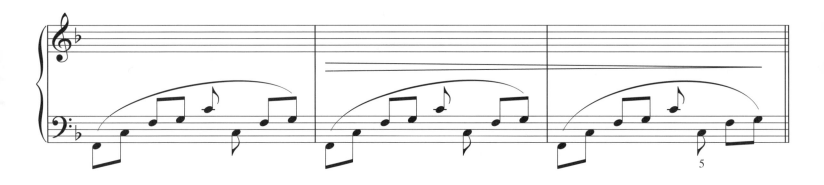

"Angels We Have Heard on High" (Traditional French Carol)

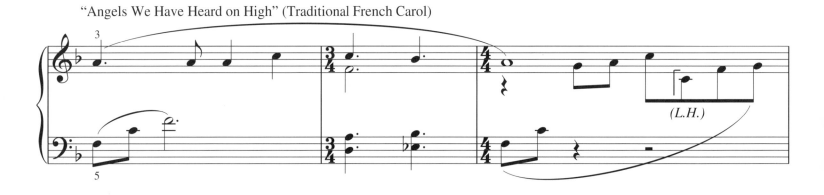

"Angels from the Realms of Glory" (Henry Smart)

Briskly (♩ = 132)

"Hark! The Herald Angels Sing" (Felix Mendelssohn)

A CHRISTMAS CELEBRATION

Arranged by Phillip Keveren

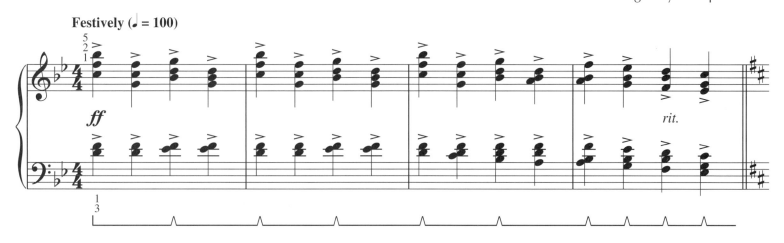

"Joy to the World" (G.F. Handel)

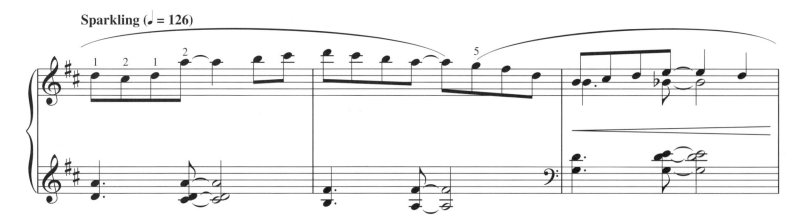

"The First Noël" (W. Sandys' *Christmas Carols*)

"Go, Tell It on the Mountain" (African-American Spiritual)

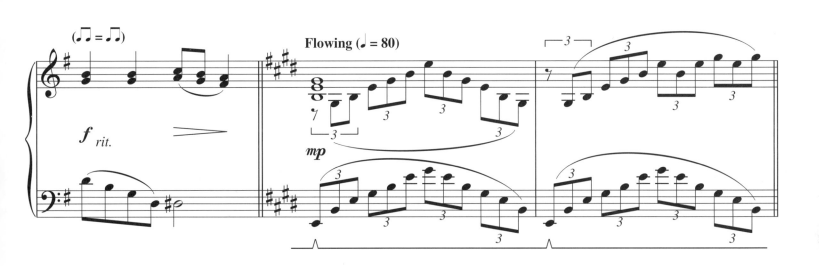

"O Come, All Ye Faithful" (John Francis Wade)

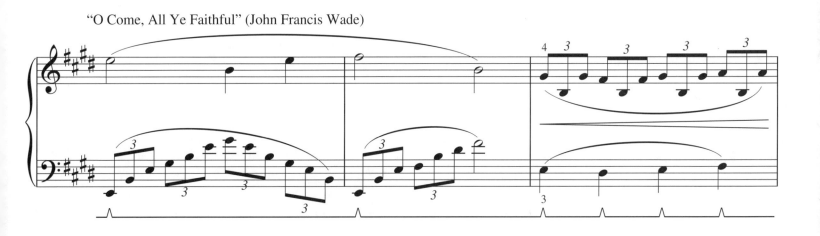

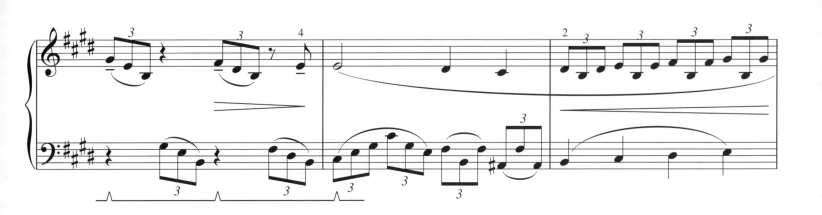

GOD REST YE MERRY, GENTLEMEN/ CAROL OF THE BELLS

Arranged by Phillip Keveren

Spirited (♩. = 120)

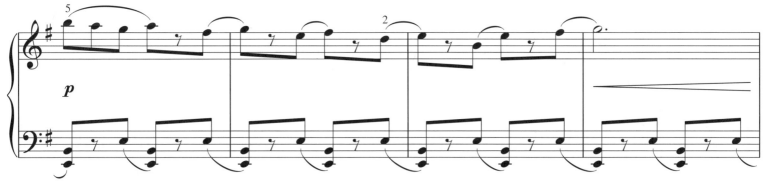

"God Rest Ye Merry, Gentlemen" (Traditional English Carol)

R.H. over L.H.

Brightly, in 'one' ($\lessdot$ = 76)

"Carol of the Bells" (Traditional Ukrainian Carol)

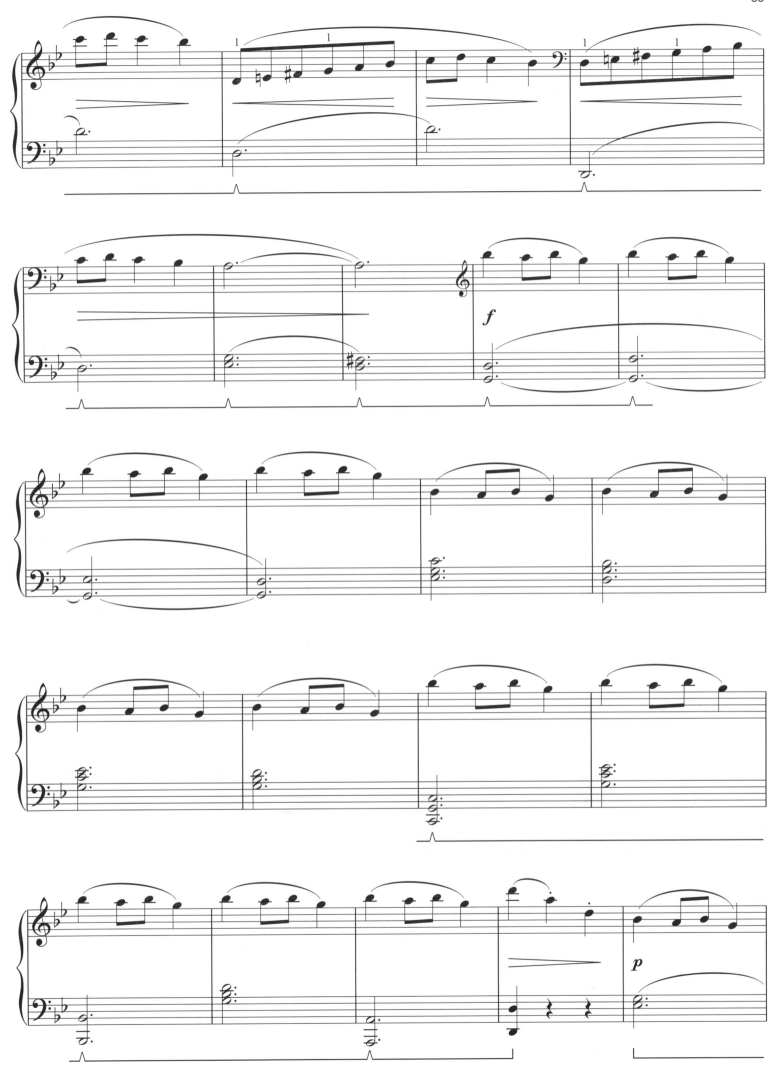

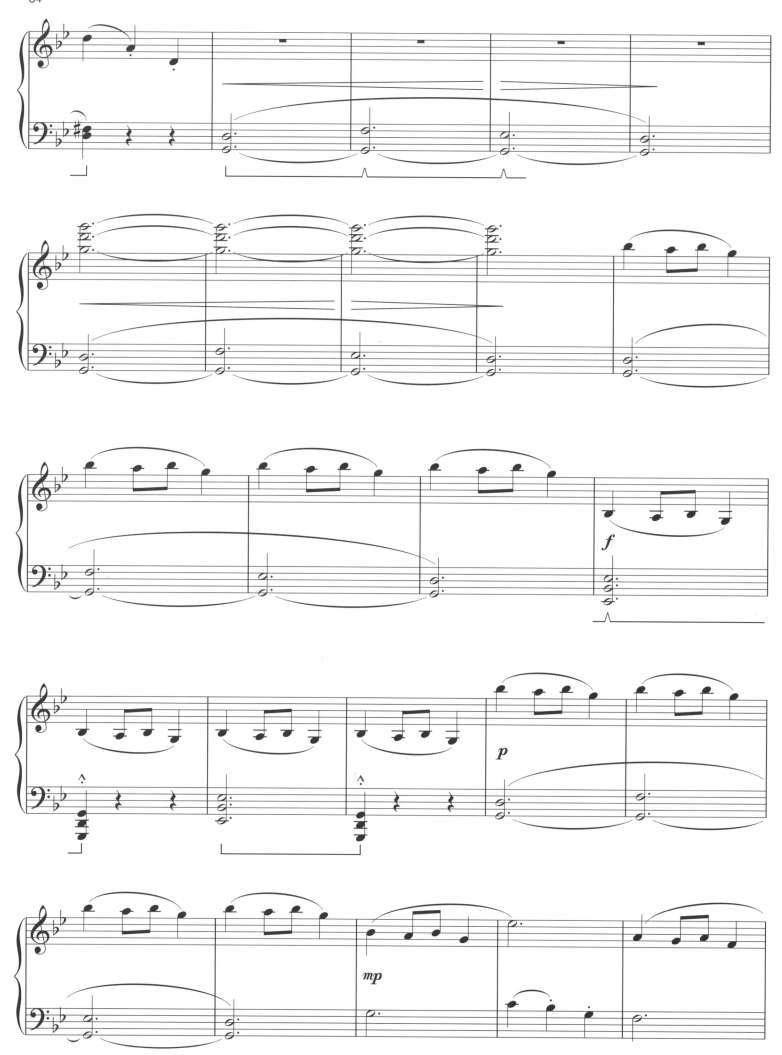

CHRISTMAS REMINISCENCE

By PHILLIP KEVEREN

Graceful Waltz (♩. = 56)

dim. e rit.

mp

poco rit.

a tempo

IT CAME UPON THE MIDNIGHT CLEAR/SILENT NIGHT

Arranged by Phillip Keveren

"It Came Upon the Midnight Clear" (Richard S. Willis)

"Silent Night" (Franz Gruber)

O HOLY NIGHT
(with "Joyful, Joyful, We Adore Thee")

Arranged by Phillip Keveren

"O Holy Night" (Adolphe Adam)

"Joyful, Joyful, We Adore Thee" (Ludwig van Beethoven)

WE THREE KINGS/
WHAT CHILD IS THIS?

Arranged by Phillip Keveren

Mysteriously (♩ = 88)

"We Three Kings" (John H. Hopkins, Jr.)

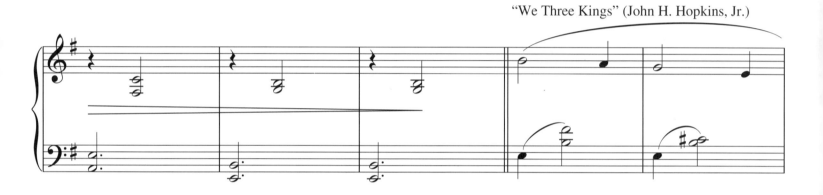

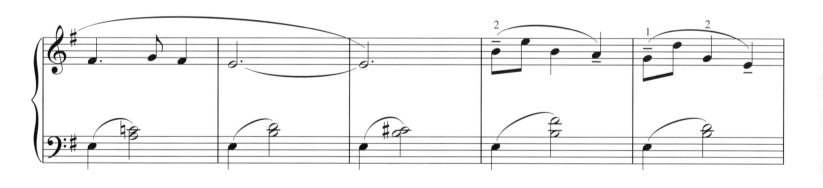

60

In 'one' (♩. = 48)

"What Child Is This?" (16th Century English Melody)

STILL, STILL, STILL
(with Brahms' "Lullaby")

Arranged by Phillip Keveren

"Still, Still, Still" (Traditional Austrian Carol)

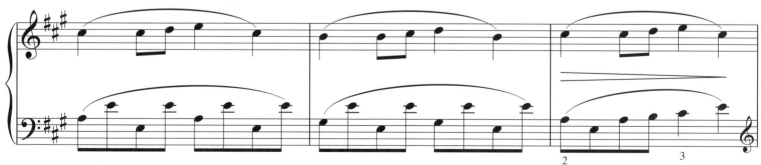

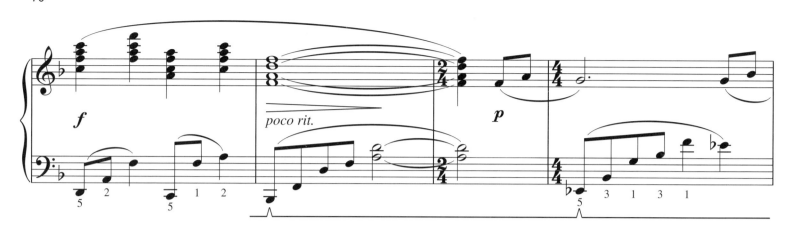

"Wiegenlied" (Johannes Brahms)

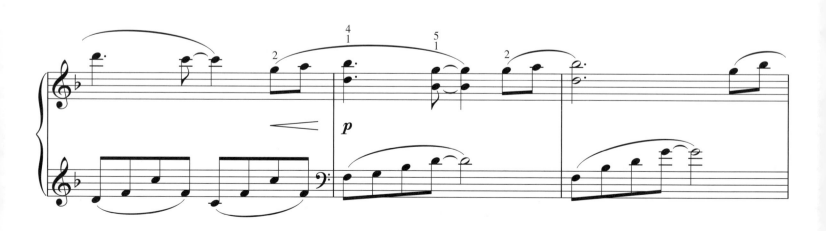